o we know it is
Spring?

Molly Aloian

 Crabtree Publishing Company

www.crabtreebooks.com

Seasons Close-Up

Author
Molly Aloian

Publishing plan research and development
Sean Charlebois, Reagan Miller
Crabtree Publishing Company

Editorial director
Kathy Middleton

Editors
Adrianna Morganelli
Crystal Sikkens

Design
Samara Parent
Margaret Amy Salter

Photo research
Samara Parent

**Production coordinator
and prepress technician**
Margaret Amy Salter

Print coordinator
Katherine Berti

Illustrations
Barbara Bedell: page 22
Katherine Berti: page 6

Photographs
Creatas: page 17
Thinkstock: page 11
All other images by Shutterstock

Library and Archives Canada Cataloguing in Publication

Aloian, Molly
    How do we know it is spring? / Molly Aloian.

(Seasons close-up)
Includes index.
Issued also in electronic formats.
ISBN 978-0-7787-0959-6 (bound).--ISBN 978-0-7787-0963-3 (pbk.)

    1. Spring--Juvenile literature. 2. Seasons--Juvenile literature.
I. Title. II. Series: Seasons close-up

QB637.5.A56 2013   j508.2   C2012-907336-9

Library of Congress Cataloging-in-Publication Data

CIP available at Library of Congress

Crabtree Publishing Company

www.crabtreebooks.com   1-800-387-7650

Printed in Canada/102013/MA20130906

Published in Canada
Crabtree Publishing
616 Welland Ave.
St. Catharines, Ontario
L2M 5V6

Published in the United States
Crabtree Publishing
PMB 59051
350 Fifth Avenue, 59th Floor
New York, New York 10118

Published in the United Kingdom
Crabtree Publishing
Maritime House
Basin Road North, Hove
BN41 1WR

Published in Australia
Crabtree Publishing
3 Charles Street
Coburg North
VIC 3058

Contents

What is spring?

In most parts of the world, there are four **seasons** in the year. The seasons repeat each year in the same pattern—spring comes before summer, summer comes before fall, fall changes to winter, and winter changes back to spring.

Each season has certain types of weather. In spring, the weather is warm and rainy.

Warmer weather

Spring is the season that comes after winter. Winter weather is cold. During winter, people usually spend a lot of time inside. When spring arrives, the weather has begun to warm up and people start spending more time outside to enjoy the warmer weather.

Why do we have spring?

Earth **rotates** around the Sun once each year. As Earth travels around the Sun, it spins on an imaginary tilted **axis**. At different times of the year, parts of Earth are tilted toward or away from the Sun as Earth rotates. This is what causes our seasons.

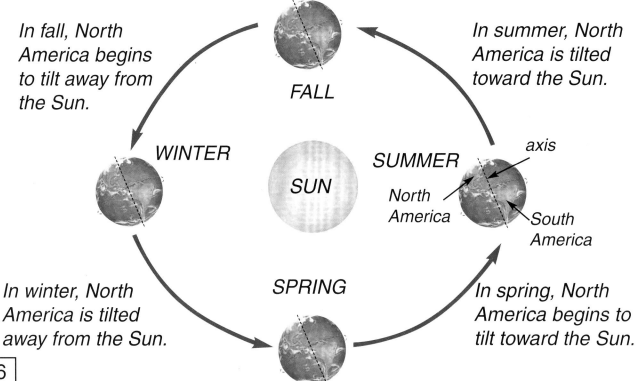

In fall, North America begins to tilt away from the Sun.

In summer, North America is tilted toward the Sun.

FALL

WINTER

SUMMER

SUN

axis

North America

South America

In winter, North America is tilted away from the Sun.

SPRING

In spring, North America begins to tilt toward the Sun.

Tilting toward

During spring in North America, the northern parts of Earth begin to tilt toward the Sun. This means that North America starts to get more hours of sunlight and warmer days.

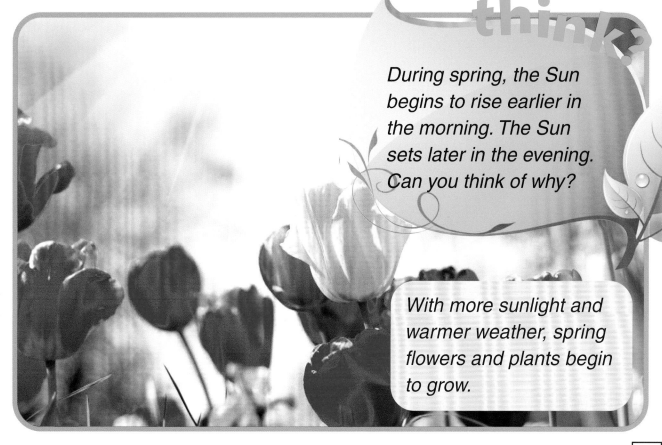

What do you think?

During spring, the Sun begins to rise earlier in the morning. The Sun sets later in the evening. Can you think of why?

With more sunlight and warmer weather, spring flowers and plants begin to grow.

When is spring?

In North America, the first day of spring is in March. Like each season, spring lasts for about three months. During this time, North America tilts closer to the Sun as South America starts to tilt away. This means the seasons in the southern parts of Earth are opposite to the seasons in the northern parts.

What do you think?

When spring begins in North America, fall is starting in South America. What month do you think fall begins in South America?

MARCH

Sunday	Monday	Tuesday	Wednesday	Thursday	Friday	Saturday
					1	2
3	4	5	6	7	8	9
10	11	12	13	14	15	16
17	18	19	20 Spring begins in North America	21	22	23
24	25	26	27	28	29	30
31						

Two instead of four

Certain parts of the world do not have spring. For example, in Mexico, there are only two seasons—the rainy season and the dry season. During the rainy season, there is heavy rain. During the dry season, there is very little rain.

What do you think?

These people in Indonesia are planting rice. Do you think they are planting the rice in the rainy season or dry season?

New life

Winter is a very cold, dark season. During winter, plants die off and many animals **hibernate**, or go into a deep sleep. Some animals **migrate**, or move to warmer places for the winter months.

Monarch butterflies migrate to warmer places in the winter. They return again in the spring.

Birds, bees, butterflies, and babies

Spring is a warmer, brighter season. New green leaves begin to grow. Hibernating animals wake up. Migrating animals return. Insects, such as bees and butterflies, start flying near new plants. Spring is also a time when new baby animals are born.

Baby birds, such as these robins, are a sign of spring.

What do you think?

Can you think of some baby animals that you have seen in the spring?

Spring weather

In spring, the weather is usually warm but not hot. The Sun feels warm, but the wind can be chilly. Strong winds blow rain clouds across the sky. In some places, there are **tornadoes** in spring. A tornado is a strong, spinning column of wind that causes a lot of damage along a small pathway.

It is best to stay in the basement of your house during a tornado.

Rainbows in spring

Spring weather is warm. Therefore, instead of snow, spring brings rain and sometimes thunderstorms. If the weather is rainy and sunny at the same time, you may see a colorful rainbow in the sky.

Plants in spring

During winter, some plants become **dormant**, or stop growing. These plants have stored food in their roots, stems, and leaves. When spring weather arrives, the plants can use the stored food to begin growing again. Other plants grow from **seeds** in spring. They use sunlight and rain to make their food as they grow.

seed

This bean plant has started to grow out of a seed.

Growing green

When the weather is warm enough, green plants begin to poke up from the ground. Bright green leaves begin to grow on trees and bushes. **Buds** begin to grow on fruit trees. Soon, the trees are covered in colorful **blossoms**.

Blossoms on fruit trees turn into fruit in the summer.

Animals in spring

This mother swan is teaching her babies how to swim and find food.

Birds build nests in spring. They lay eggs in the nests. Baby birds hatch from the eggs. Mother birds must teach their babies how to fly. Mother ducks teach their ducklings how to swim in ponds and creeks.

Baby animals

Some baby animals do not hatch from eggs. They are born live in the spring. This is because the weather is warm and there are plenty of plant foods. Some animals give birth to only one baby a year. Other animals have many babies between spring and fall.

In the woods, mother deer give birth to fawns.

Springing to action

After the cold of winter, it is fun to play outside on a sunny spring day. Many people go on hikes or nature walks. It is fun to look for plant buds and baby animals. Some people fly kites on windy spring days. Others jump rope or play hopscotch.

Hopscotch is a fun game to play outside with your friends.

What do you think?

Think of your favorite spring activity. What kind of clothes do you wear for the activity?

Spring suit

The weather can change quickly in spring. For example, it can be sunny one hour and rainy the next hour. When going outdoors, many people bring umbrellas in case the weather changes. Raincoats and boots are also important spring clothing.

Planting in spring

In spring, many people like to plant gardens. They plant flower or vegetable gardens in their yards so they can watch the plants grow. Warm spring weather and rain make garden plants grow quickly.

These plants will grow vegetables on them in the summer.

Spring foods

Spring is an important time for farmers. Many farmers plant food crops in spring. They plant fruits and vegetables such as corn. Crops that are planted in spring are usually **harvested** in the late summer or fall.

What do you think?

Many fruits grow on trees. Can you think of a fruit that grows on trees?

This farmer is planting corn in the spring.

21

Spying on spring

This activity will help you track all the changes that are taking place around you during spring. You will need:

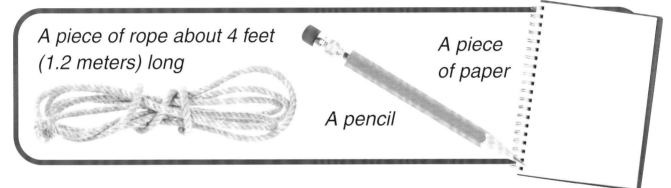

A piece of rope about 4 feet (1.2 meters) long

A pencil

A piece of paper

Ask an adult to help you tie the ends of the rope together to make a circle. Choose a spot in your yard and lay the circle of rope on the ground. Be sure to choose a spot that people do not walk across. Visit the spot every day and write down any changes you notice.

Is the ground wet or dry?
Which plants are poking
through the ground?
What insects do you see?

Learning more

Books

Everything Spring (Picture the Seasons) by Jill Esbaum.
National Geographic Children's Books, 2010.

Spring Surprises (Step into Reading) by Anna Jane Hays.
Random House Books for Young Readers, 2010.

What Is Weather? (Weather Close-Up) by Robin Johnson.
Crabtree Publishing Company, 2012.

Which Season Is It? (My World) by Bobbie Kalman.
Crabtree Publishing Company, 2011.

Websites

Changing Seasons—Exploring Nature Educational Resource
www.exploringnature.org/db/detail.php?dbID=112&detID=2634

Spring Activities for Kids
www.activityvillage.co.uk/spring.htm

Science projects: ideas, topics, methods, and examples
www.sciencemadesimple.com/

Seasons—Science for Kids!
www.historyforkids.org/scienceforkids/physics/weather/seasons.htm

Words to know

axis (AK-sis) noun The straight line around which Earth rotates

blossoms (BLOS-uhm) noun The flowers on a tree or other plant

bud (buhd) noun A small growth that develop on the tip of a stem or branch

dormant (DAWR-muhnt) adjective Not active or growing

harvest (HAHR-vist) verb To gather or collect a crop

hibernate (HI-ber-neyt) verb To go through winter in a sleeping or resting state

migrate (MAHY-greyt) verb Moving from one place to another for warmer weather or food

rotate (ROH-teyt) verb To spin or move in a circle around something

season (SEE-zuhn) noun A period of time with certain temperatures and weather

seed (SEED) noun The part of an adult plant that will grow into new plants

tornado (tawr-NEY-doh) noun A very strong column of wind that blow over narrow paths of land

A noun is a person, place, or thing. A verb is an action word that tells you what someone or something does. An adjective is a word that tells you what something is like.

Index